STUDIES ON THE LOGIC OF AUTOMATIC COMPUTATION

(Incremental Data Assimilation in

Man - Computer Systems)

by Lionello A. Lombardi

Working Paper 10-63

STUDIES ON THE LOGIC OF AUTOMATIC COMPUTATION

(Incremental Data Assimilation in Man - Computer Systems)

by Lionello A. Lombardi

Massachusetts Institute of Technology

SUMMARY

The main problem of modern computation theory and methodology arises from the fact that conventional digital computers, developed following the classical ideas of Turing and von Neumann, fail to meet many requirements as components or terminals of complex man-computer information system textures. Their main limitation in such context is sometimes identified as their exceedingly high needs regarding the specificity of both the algorithms that they can accept for execution, and their data, which makes them not primarily suitable as organs for incremental data assimilation through adaptively growing and incrementally modifiable algorithms. Accordingly, basic research is being carried out on designing new foundations for the logic of automatic digital computation.

This paper consists of two preliminary probes into the idea of the "incremental declarative computer" as basis for a possible solution to this problem. The first part is devoted to developing the syntax of a programming language for such computer based on a revision of Karl Menger's notation. Though it has been recently decided to discard this notation and replace it by a substantially new one, to which the human is more immediately responsive, still

this first part should be considered as an early version of the first chapter of the book devoted to the development of a new computation philosophy, that this author is writing. The second part (corresponding to the second chapter of the book) presents a new kind of memory organization based on the ideas of Newell, Shaw and Simon, but where such ideas are revised in a way to enable the computer to scan symbolic expressions imbedded in lists right to left (i.e., in the extended Lukasiewicz sense), which would not be easy if the IPLV, LISP or FLPL list-structured memory organization were adopted.

There are here no hints to the other chapters, devoted to the design of the control unit of the new computer and recursive functions of symbolic expressions, its input-output system, algorithms to co-ordinate the information flow, random accessing and information retrieval, and identification of parameters to describe computer systems quantitatively, respectively.

Cambridge, Massachusetts

January 30, 1963

L. A. [illegible]

CHAPTER I SYNTAX

General

This chapter is devoted to introducing a primitive alphabet of marks, establishing rules by means of which marks can be assembled to form those particular aggregates -- the forms -- which are the basis for the definition of the functions that the abstract computer can compute, studying properties of such forms, such as the possibility of their canonical decomposition within the space of all forms, and discussing the detachment operation which transforms any ordered couple of forms into a third one. Detachment is the basic operation of this theory, the semantics being defined in terms of recursive detachments. The most important property is [illegible], which is proved here in the most general form.

The alphabet presented in this chapter is restricted to a preliminary set of marks sufficient for introducing formation rules and elementary evaluation methods. Later on the alphabet will be extended in order to allow for more compact representation of functions and more general evaluation methods.

Section 1.1 Primitive Alphabet

The primitive alphabet consists of three kinds of marks: constants, operative marks and punctuation marks.

Constants may be of four kinds: integers, rationals (represented as finite sequences of decimal digits with a decimal point), truth valued or alphanumeric. Integers and rationals may be signed, and whenever they are not they are taken to be positive. Alphanumeric constants consist of finite sequences of capital Roman characters and decimal digits, at least one being of the first kind. For example, [illegible] and [illegible] are integer constants, [illegible] and [illegible] are rational constants while REAL[illegible] or [illegible] are alphanumeric constants. There will be only two truth values, namely [illegible] and [illegible]. Constants being a well established concept in computation there is no reason to discuss them further here.

There are six operative marks in the primitive alphabet: [illegible], [illegible], [illegible], [illegible], [illegible] and [illegible], called variable mark, function mark, system function mark, direct function mark, true condition mark and false condition mark, respectively.

The first three of them will be used to define the three types of aggregates of marks, which are variable, function letter and system function letter, respectively. The direct function mark will be used to control the evaluation of forms which, instead of being retrieved from the library, are either introduced as part of the data or are generated during computation. Lastly, both condition marks will be used in connection with functions which are represented by different forms in different portions of their domain of definition.

Punctuation marks are the comma, the colon and the left and right parentheses.

Section 1.2 Forms

Any ordered finite sequence of atoms, with or without recurrences of the atoms is called an aggregate.

A particular kind of aggregates, referred to as forms, play a most important role and need a thorough discussion. The first and simplest kinds of forms are those covered by the following.

Definition 1. Constants and connective marks are forms.

It should be noticed that punctuation marks are not forms according to this first definition. [illegible] are forms. An aggregate which can be proved to be a form on the basis of definition 1 alone will be referred to as primary form or atom.

If a and b are two aggregates, the aggregate ab will be called concatenation of a and b. Clearly concatenation is an associative but not commutative operation.

Definition 2. The concatenation of two forms is a form.

Let $a_1, a_2, \ldots, a_n$ be atoms. Then, by a total of $(n-1)$ instances of definitions 1 and 2 it can be proved that the aggregate

$$a_1 a_2 \ldots a_n \quad (1)$$

is a form. Vice versa, any aggregate which can be proved to be a form only by applying definitions 1 and 2 a finite number of times, has the structure (1), where a_i are atoms and n is an integer.

[illegible]

For example,

(x) (3a)

(-3 ABS, [illegible]) (3b)

(x, 2.(-3 ABS, y, 2.)) (3c)

are forms.

Let us now associate to each form an integer, called level, as follows:

The level of an atom is 0

The level of a form a obtained by concatenation of two other forms a_1 and a_2 is the largest of the levels of a_1 and a_2

The level of a form a_1 obtained by enclosing in parentheses the form a_2 of level j is j + 1

For example,

x, 3

is a form of level 0,

(f), SUM, (2), 3.14, -7

is a form of level 1 and

((1), SUM, 3.14, (12.5 x.7))

is a form of level 2.

Definition 4. (recursion clause) No aggregate is a form unless its being a form follows from a finite number of instances of definitions 1, 2 and 3.

For example, neither x(nor ff nor (5 are forms, because one can

only prove that no finite sequence of instances of definitions 1, 2, 3 could prove them to be forms.

Definition 4 says that, for each aggregate which is a form, there must be at least one proof, that will be called *structural proof*, of its being so, consisting of a finite sequence of instances of definitions 1, 2 and 3, such that each instance of definition 1 is always applied to a constant or an operative mark and each instance of definition 2 and 3 is applied to the concatenation or enclosure in parentheses, respectively, of aggregates which have been proved to be forms as result of instances of definitions 1, 2 or 3 preceding it in such proof. We shall always assume that the last statement of any structural proof of an expression e states e being a form.

Consider subsequences of statements of a structural proof of e consisting of statements each of which, excluding the first, applies to at least one aggregate which is stated to be a form by the preceding statement of the subsequence, and whose last statement is the last one of the structural proof. If a statement does not belong to any such subsequence, it is evidently irrelevant to the proof. We shall always assume that structural proofs do not contain such irrelevant statements.
The number of occurrences of marks in an aggregate e is denoted $L(e)$.
An aggregate consisting of the first n occurrences of marks of a form having at least n occurrences of marks is referred to as *partial form*.

Section 1.3 Properties of Forms

Let us first consider the following

Lemma 1: The difference between the total number of occurrences of open and closed parentheses in a form is always 0.

Proof: Obvious, by definition 4, section 1.2. In fact, the only provision for introducing parentheses in the structural proof of a form is given by definition 4, section 1.2, which requires introduction of parentheses in couples of an open one and a closed one.

Let now e be an aggregate, and let a be an occurrence of a mark different from a parenthesis in e. Let $O_l(a,e)$ and $C_l(a,e)$ denote the total number of occurrences of open and closed parentheses, respectively, to the left of a in e and $O_r(a,e)$ and $C_r(a,e)$ the total number of occurrences of open and closed parentheses, respectively, to the right of a in e. Let us prove the following

Theorem 2: If e is a form, then for each a,

$$O_l(a,e) - C_l(a,e) = C_r(a,e) - O_r(a,e) \qquad (1)$$

Proof: by induction with respect to the level n of e. First of all, (1) is true for $n = 0$, because in this case (e) has the format (1) of section 1.2, where all e_i are atoms, and there are no occurrences of parentheses. Assume now that the theorem has been proved for all integers t such that $0 \leq t < n$ and let us consider, in a structural proof of e, the first instance

of Definition 2 or 3, Section 1.2, [illegible] an aggregate, say e', containing e in a form of [illegible] consists of the enclosure in parentheses of [illegible] of level $n-1$, or because e' is the result of [illegible] of two forms e_1' and e_2', one of which, say e_2', has level n while the other, say e_1', contains e and has level [illegible] of the proof cannot contain instances of [illegible] 1.2, applied to [illegible] containing e' as part, because otherwise e would be of a level greater than n. Consequently, e has the structure

$$e_1 . e_2 \ldots e' \ldots e_{q-1} e_q \qquad (2)$$

where e' is either

$$e_1' . e_2' \qquad (3)$$

or

$$(e_1') \qquad (4)$$

In both cases

$$C_r(e, e_1') - C_r(e, e_1') = C_r(e, e_1') - C_r(e, e_1') \qquad (5)$$

by hypothesis. The contribution of e_2' and of all e_i different from e' to both members of (1) vanishes by Lemma 1, while the parentheses enclosing e_1' in the second case contribute one unit to both members of (1), so that, in the second case,

$$C_r(e, e) - C_r(e, e) = C_r(e, e_1') - C_r(e, e_1') + 1 \qquad (6a)$$

and

$$C_r(e, e) - C_r(e, e) = C_r(e, e_1') - C_r(e, e_1') + 1 \qquad (7a)$$

and (1) follows by subtraction of (7a) from (6a) and application

or (2). In the first case there are the relations

$$O_r(a,e) - C_r(a,e) = O_r(a,e^*_1) - C_r(a,e^*_1) \qquad (6b)$$

$$O_l(a,e) - C_l(a,e) = O_l(a,e^*_1) - C_l(a,e^*_1) \qquad (7b)$$

and the conclusion follows similarly. The theorem is thus proved.

Theorem 3a): If e is a form, then, for all a

$$O_l(a,e) \leq C_l(a,e) \qquad (8a)$$

Proof. Again (8a) is true if the level n of e is 0. Let us repeat the hypotheses and reasoning of the proof of theorem 2 until the point of defining the forms (2), (3) and (4).

In both cases

$$O_l(a,e^*_1) \leq C_l(a,e^*_1)$$

by hypothesis. The contribution of e^*_2 and of all e_i different from e^* to both members of (8a) vanishes by lemma 1, [illegible].

In the second case, the occurrence of an open parenthesis limiting e^*_1 to the left contributes a unit to the left member of (8a) and none to the right one. From this point the proof follows like the one of theorem 2.

Analogously one can prove

Theorem 3b): If e is a form, then, for all a,

$$O_r(a,e) \leq C_r(a,e) \qquad (8b)$$

Let a and b be aggregates, and let a be another aggregate consisting of a sequence of consecutive occurrences of marks in e. Then the aggregate obtained by replacing b for a in e will be called substitute of b for a in e and denoted $S(b,a,e)$

Theorem 4: If c and b are forms and a is an occurrence of an atom in c then S(b,a,c) is a form.

Proof: Let g be the atom occurring in a. Consider, in any one structural proof of c, the instance of definition 1, section 1.2, stating that g is a form, and insert right after the above occurrence a structural proof of b. Then replace graphically b for g in all statements of the structural proof following such insertion, and then remove all irrelevant statements from the result, if there are some. The resulting sequence of statements is a structural proof of S(b,a,c) which is therefore a form.

The reason for keeping the statement that g is a form instead of simply replacing it with a structural proof of b is that there might be occurrences of g in c other than a.

So far the concept of level of a form has been envisaged as dependent of the proof that one can give that an aggregate is such. This proof is not necessarily unique, and it is easy to give examples where more than one proof is possible. Consequently, the level is not a priori unique, but it is necessary for further development to give a proof of its uniqueness. Before doing this, however, it is handy to introduce a new concept: we shall call left depth and right depth, respectively, of the occurrence of a mark a different from a parenthesis in an

aggregate $\underline{s}$ the integers

$$D_\lambda(\underline{s},\underline{e}) = C_\lambda(\underline{s},\underline{e}) - C_\rho(\underline{s},\underline{e}) \qquad (9a)$$

and

$$D_\rho(\underline{s},\underline{e}) = C_\rho(\underline{s},\underline{e}) - C_\lambda(\underline{s},\underline{e}) \qquad (9b)$$

By theorem 3, neither depth is ever negative when $\underline{e}$ is a form.

Theorem 5. The maximum depth of occurrences of atoms in a form $\underline{e}$ is the level of $\underline{e}$.

The main consequence of this theorem is the fact that it provides a guarantee of the uniqueness of the level of any form.

Proof: Notice first that each occurrence of definition 1, section 1.2 yields a form of level 0, which therefore has no occurrences of parentheses and whose only atom has consequently depth 0. Each occurrence of definition 2, section 1.2, yields forms where the maximum level of occurrences of atoms is the maximum of the ones of the forms which are concatenated; in fact, by lemma 1 applied to any two forms $\underline{e}_1$ and $\underline{e}_2$, the concatenation of e_1 and e_2 does not yield any change in the depth of any occurrence of atoms in either $\underline{e}_1$ or $\underline{e}_2$. Each occurrence of definition 3, section 1.2, increases by one the depth of all affected occurrences of atoms. Then all three definitions yield the same generation or variation both of maximum depth and level. This applies in particular to any sequence of occurrences of definitions 1, 2 and 3, section 1.2, constituting a structural proof of $\underline{e}$; hence the theorem.

If <u>a</u> denotes an aggregate, let <u>a</u>$^{-1}$ denote the <u>inverse</u> aggregate of <u>a</u> consisting of the occurrences of marks which compose <u>a</u>, but in the reverse order and whose open parentheses are replaced by closed ones in all of their occurrences, and vice versa. Then there subsists the following

<u>Theorem 6: If a is a form, so is a^{-1}</u>

<u>Proof:</u> In fact, a structural proof for a^{-1} can be constructed by simply inverting the order of all couples of forms which are concatenated by occurrences of definition 2, section 1.2., in the structural proof of <u>a</u>.

Section 1.[illegible] Canonical Decomposition

Let g be a form of level n and let us define the canonical decomposition of g, [illegible] writing g as

$$g_1 \; C_0 \; \ldots \; C_0 \; g_{M(g)} \qquad (1.[illegible])$$

where each g_i is an aggregate, called i-th canonical element of g, and $M(g)$ is a positive integer, called number of canonical elements of g. The canonical decomposition of g is based on the occurrences of connectives of depth 0 in g. If there are no such occurrences, then $M(g) = 1$ and the canonical decomposition of g is g, and g is said to be undecomposable. If there are $p-1$ such occurrences, then $M(g) = p$, [illegible] g_1 and $g_{M(g)}$ are the aggregates consisting of all occurrences of marks preceding the first of such occurrences or following the last of them, respectively, while g_i ($i = 2, \ldots, M(g)-1$) is the aggregate consisting of all occurrences of marks following the $(i-1)$-th and preceding the i-th of such occurrences.

The canonical decomposition thus defined is obviously unique. In the case $M(g) > 1$, however, it remains to prove the following.

Theorem 1 (Canonical Decomposition Theorem). The canonical components of a form are forms.

Proof: Let us prove this theorem for the canonical component g_1. If g_1 consists of a constant or [illegible] the result is immediate. Otherwise, let us consider a structural proof of g, and observe that it must contain the statement that g_1 is a form. Let t be the first non-[illegible] statement (see section 1.[illegible] of the [illegible]

of such structural proof stating that an aggregate e^* containing c_1 is a form. There must be an occurrence of a comma of depth 0 either to the left or to the right of c_1 in e, and let us call it c. Let us show that c^* and e_1 are identical, which would prove the theorem. In fact, suppose they were not: In this case t cannot be an instance of definition 3, section 1.2. because, if it were, c could no longer have depth 0 in e. Therefore, t is an occurrence of definition 2. stating that e^* is a form because it is the concatenation of two forms e^*_1 or e^*_2. Let us call c^* the occurrence of a comma linking such concatenation, which must be in e_1, otherwise either e^*_1 or e^*_2 would contain e_1, and t would not be the first statement yielding a form containing e_1. Furthermore c^* must have depth 0 in e^*. Let us show that c^* has also depth 0 in e. In fact, each statement of the structural proof of e raising the depth of c^* would also raise the one of c, and c^* and c must consequently have the same depth in e, which is 0. But e_1 cannot contain commas of depth 0 in e, which ends the proof of the theorem.

Section 1.5 Partial [illegible]

Let me call *variable letter* a form of level 1 consisting of the enclosure in parentheses of the concatenation of the variable mark x and a positive integer called *subscript*. For example, the form

$$(x,8) \qquad (1)$$

is a variable letter.

The approach taken here requires developing morphology and syntax before introducing any semantical elements. Consequently, it is impossible so far to assign a meaning to any notation. However, a smooth acquaintance with the language of the abstract computer should be improved by reading the variable letter (x,n) in the following way: "the n th variable". For example, (1) should be read "the eighth variable".

A form a where no variable letter (x,r) ever occurs unless, for all integers i such that $0 < i < r$, there is in a at least one occurrence of the variable letter (x,i) is called a *compact* form. In the sequel it will become clear that the use of compact forms is a protection against uncontrolled growing of the subscripts of variable letters while computations progress.

Let a and b be [illegible] and let v be an occurrence of a variable letter in a. We have the following

Theorem 1: $S(b,v,a)$ is an form.

Proof. In fact the structural proof of a must contain the statement that the variable letter occurring in v is a form; this can be proved with a technique at all similar to the one used to prove the canonical decomposition theorem, section 1.4, that is, by considering the first non-[illegible] statement t stating that a form g* containing v is a form. g cannot obviously be an instance of definition 1, section 1.2, and if g* differs from the form occurring in v it could not be an instance of definition 2, same section, because if it were one of the two concatenated forms would have an occurrence in [illegible] forms of negative depth. Nor can g be an instance of definition 3, same section, because if it were it would enclose in parentheses an aggregate already containing v. From this point, the proof follows like the one of theorem 4, section 1.3.

This proof can immediately be extended to the case where v is an occurrence of any undecomposable form. In contrast, if such form has several components, this proof would no longer hold. The theorem would still be true but should be proved in a different way.

If a is a form, the largest of all values of the subscripts of the variable letters of a will be denoted $H(a)$.

Let a and b be forms, and suppose that

$$H(a) = H(b) \qquad (2)$$

Suppose further that b has a total of k, $(k \geq 0)$, occurrences of

variable letters. Let us serialize such occurrences left to right by [illegible] (x, i_r) denote the variable letter [illegible] a new form obtained from [illegible] the new variable letter [illegible] the i_r-th [illegible] a. This new form is called **partial detachment of** [illegible] **b** and denoted

$$(b \,|_p\, a)$$

By Theorem 1, the partial detachment of two forms is a form. Furthermore,

$$N((b \,|_p\, a)) = N(b) \qquad (3)$$

and

$$H((b \,|_p\, a)) = H(b) - H(a) + H(a) \qquad (4)$$

For example, let a be [illegible] be $(x, 3)$, [illegible] and $(b \,|_p\, a)$ is [illegible], 2, [illegible]

Notice that the partial detachment of a compact form from another compact form is also a compact form, that is, partial detachment operation preserves compactness.

Another property of partial detachment is that there can be two occurrences of a single variable letter in $(b \,|_p\, a)$ iff they are both the result of replacing two occurrences of a single variable letter which originally were contained either both in a or both in b. In other terms, partial detachment operation preserves the notational distinction of variable letters.

Let us prove the following

Theorem 2 (Partial associativity theorem). If a, b, c are forms such that both partial substitutions $(a \,;_p (b \,;_p c))$ and $((c \,;_p b) \,;_p a)$ exist and if

$$[illegible] \qquad (5)$$

then

$$[illegible] = ((c \,;_p b) \,;_p a) \qquad (6)$$

Proof: If c does not contain occurrences of variable letters the theorem is true because, for all forms d, $(c \,;_p d) = c$. Otherwise, the two members of (6) are both obtained from c by merely replacing all occurrences of variable letters, and the theorem should be proved by showing that such replacements are identical in both cases. Let v be such an occurrence, say of the variable letter (g, i). In computing the left member of (6), v is replaced by the g-th canonical component of $(b \,; a)$, which is obtained from the g-th canonical component b_g of b by replacing each occurrence of a variable letter (g, j), such that $j \geq M(g)$, by $(x, j - M(a) + M(g))$, and each occurrence of any other variable letter (g, h) by the g-th canonical component a_h of a. In computing the right member of (6), v is first replaced by b_i, and then each occurrence of a function letter (z, k) within this replacement is replaced by $(z, k - M(z) + M(g))$ or by a_k, depending on whether or not $k \geq M(g)$. In this case the results are obviously identical because they come from the same action taken on the same

data, which are simply differently located when the action is taken.

Consider now the case $\underline{i} > M(\underline{b})$. In this case, in order to compute the left member of (6), $\underline{v}$ is replaced by $(\underline{x}, \underline{i}-M(\underline{b}|\underline{a}) + H(\underline{b}\,|_p\,\underline{a}))$, that is by $(\underline{x}, \underline{i}-M(\underline{b}) + H(\underline{b}) + H(\underline{a})-M(\underline{a}))$, while in order to compute the right member of (6) it is first replaced by $(\underline{x}, \underline{i}-M(\underline{b}) + H(\underline{b}))$, to compute $(a\,|_p\,b)$; then, because of (4), it is finally replaced by $(\underline{x}, \underline{i} -M(\underline{b}) + H(\underline{b})-M(\underline{a}) + H(\underline{a}))$. These replacements are identical, and the theorem is thus proved.

[illegible]

[illegible]

[illegible] the form consisting of the [illegible]

element of [illegible]

whether [illegible]

[illegible]

occurrence of [illegible]

and [illegible]

[illegible]

[illegible]

[illegible]

[illegible]

on the above [illegible]

[illegible]

for [illegible]

operator [illegible] mapping of [illegible]

all forms into the space of [illegible]

called *determinant* [illegible] the result [illegible]

[illegible]

[illegible]

Whatever [illegible] section [illegible]

[illegible]

that is, detachment is a generalization of partial detachment. It should also be noted that detachment preserves completeness and notational distinction of variable letters.

Detachment plays a dominant role in the definition of the abstract computer. From its standpoint computation consists basically of sequences of detachments of forms and preparation for such detachments. The ability to detach is the basic feature of the abstract computer. The relevance of detachment is revealed by a property whose importance goes far beyond the importance of the two other properties already observed, namely, preservation of completeness and of notational distinction of variable letters. This property is associativity. Associativity of detachment is at the basis of the unitary approach to all forms of computation obtained through the abstract computer. It makes compilation and manipulation of them possible. It allows for [illegible] alternate, possibly rather deceptive theories [illegible] abstract computation can be described by various other definitions of this operation, which, however, should always be [illegible]. If two theories of computation or abstract computers admit a one-to-one correspondence between the forms they consider which is preserved by the respective detachments, that is, if they are isomorphic under detachment, they should be considered identical. When (as this author hopes for the future) there will be a wealth of very [illegible] mathematical theory of computation or abstract computers, each one of them will be defined and characterized by

the definition of its detachment operation.

For most practical purposes, in this particular theory, detachment is useful when (2), section 1.5, is satisfied, and its associativity is utilized only under the hypotheses of theorem 2, section 1.5, which also allow for a trivial proof. However, for the sake of completeness, this section is devoted to defining this basic detachment operation and to proving its associativity in the most general case, that is, to proving the following

Theorem 1 (Associativity Theorem) If *a*, *b* and *c* are forms, then

$$(c \mid (b \mid a)) = ((c \mid b) \mid a) \qquad (1)$$

Proof: Let *t* be a non-negative integer, and let Q(*t*) denote the infinite sequence of variable letters, separated by commas

$$(x, t+1),\ (x, t+2),\ (x, t+3), \ldots\ldots\ldots\ldots \qquad (2)$$

Let *c* be a form, and let *c'* denote the sequence of forms, separated by commas, whose first N(*c*) elements are the canonical components of *c*, and the following are the elements of the sequence Q(N(*c*)). For *i* > N(*c*), consequently, the *i*-th element of *c'* is $(x, N(c)-N(c)+i)$. Sequences obtained from forms like *c'* will be called *infinite forms* and *c'* will be called the *infinite extension* of *c*.

The formalization of this concept can immediately be obtained, for example, by imbedding infinite forms into the class of infinite sequences of marks obtained by replacing "finite or infinite" for "finite" in definition 4, section 1.2. The concept of canonical

element of $L(\underline{c},\underline{r})$ and $M(\underline{c},\underline{r})$ can be immediately extended to infinite forms.

Let now $\underline{g}$ be a form or an infinite form and let $s(\underline{g})$ be the smallest non-negative integer $\underline{i}$, such that

$$M(\underline{g},\underline{i}) = G(L(\underline{g},\underline{i}))$$

We will then call contraction of $\underline{g}$ and denote $\ddot{\underline{g}}$ the form

$$L(\underline{g},s(\underline{g}))$$

If two forms $\underline{a}$ and $\underline{b}$ have identical infinite extensions, they have also identical contractions and will be called similar. The similarity relation of forms, denoted $\underline{a} \sim \underline{b}$, is reflexive, commutative and transitive, and classes of equivalence under such relation can be represented by either the common infinite extension or the common contraction of their members. The components of a form $\underline{a}$ which are not also components of $\ddot{\underline{a}}$ will be called trailed components or dummy components of $\underline{a}$. Two similar forms can only differ by the number of trailed components.

If $\underline{a}$ and $\underline{b}$ are contracted forms, that is, forms without trailed components, then $(\underline{b}|\underline{a})$ is also contracted.

If $\underline{a}$, $\underline{b}$ and $\underline{c}$ are forms such that $\underline{a} \sim \underline{b}$, then

$$(\underline{a}|\underline{c}) \sim (\underline{b}|\underline{c}) \qquad (3)$$

and

$$(\underline{c}|\underline{a}) \sim (\underline{c}|\underline{b}) \qquad (4)$$

Now let $\underline{c}$ and $\underline{d}$ be infinite forms. The partial detachment

$$(\underline{c}\;|_{p}\underline{d})$$

is defined like in section 1.5 for forms, with the only difference that the limitation (2), section 1.5, does not apply in this

case. Partial detachment of infinite forms is not only always defined, but also evidently associative, as can be proved by repeating the first part of Theorem 2, section 1.5. Furthermore, for any two forms $\underline{a}$ and $\underline{b}$,

$$\overline{(\underline{a}|\underline{b})} = (\overline{\underline{a}}\,|\,\overline{\underline{b}})$$

Then, for any three forms $\underline{a}$, $\underline{b}$ and $\underline{c}$

$$\overline{(\underline{c}|(\underline{b}|\underline{a}))} = (\overline{\underline{c}}\,|\,\overline{(\underline{b}|\underline{a})}) = (\overline{\underline{c}}\,|\,(\overline{\underline{b}}\,|\,\overline{\underline{a}})) =$$
$$((\overline{\underline{c}}\,|\,\overline{\underline{b}})\,|\,\overline{\underline{a}}) = (\overline{(\underline{c}|\underline{b})}\,|\,\overline{\underline{a}}) = \overline{((\underline{c}|\underline{b})|\underline{a})}$$

Hence, by contracting,

$$(\underline{c}|(\underline{b}|\underline{a})) \sim ((\underline{c}|\underline{b})|\underline{a}) \qquad (5)$$

We must now prove that the two members of (5) have the same number of trailed components, that is, that they are equal. In order to do so, let us denote α a constant which never occurs in $\underline{a}$, $\underline{b}$, or $\underline{c}$, and let us call $\underline{a}^*$, $\underline{b}^*$ and $\underline{c}^*$ the new forms obtained by substituting for each trailed component, say (x, i), of $\underline{a}$, $\underline{b}$ or $\underline{c}$, respectively, the form

$$(\alpha, (x, i)). \qquad (6)$$

The forms $\underline{a}^*$, $\underline{b}^*$ and $\underline{c}^*$ are contracted, and, by replacing them for $\underline{a}$, $\underline{b}$ and $\underline{c}$, respectively, in (5), since the detachment of contracted forms is contracted, we obtain

$$(\underline{c}^*|(\underline{b}^*|\underline{a}^*)) = ((\underline{c}^*|\underline{b}^*)|\underline{a}^*) \qquad (7)$$

Let us now replace $(\underline{x}, \underline{i})$ for all corresponding forms of the type (6) contained in (7). Because of the way α was chosen, this replacement transforms the left and right member of (7) into $(\underline{c}|(\underline{b}|\underline{a}))$ and $((\underline{c}|\underline{b})|\underline{a})$, respectively; hence (1), and the theorem is completely proved.

Remark. The proof of the associativity theorem given in this section, which is based on an isomorphism, is simple but has the disadvantage of implicitly requiring the postulate of the existence of a space of sets of denumerably many marks, that is, sets of power $\aleph_0$. This postulate cannot be represented in any formalism, and consequently one could a priori think that associativity holds only provided that the denumerable space of forms is imbedded in an appropriate space of power $\aleph_1$. In order to show that associativity holds independently of such imbedding, one should prove it independently of the above postulate, that is, one should give a proof in the finite of associativity. However, this logical point not falling within the scope of this work, it will not here be the object of further elaboration.

Remark 2: Let Ω be the empty expression (which can be represented, for example, by $(\underline{x}, 1)$, which is similar to it.) Then for all forms $\underline{a}$

$$(\Omega | \underline{a}) \sim \underline{a}$$

and

$$(\underline{a} | \Omega) \sim \underline{a}$$

In other words, if we consider the family of all classes of equivalence by similarity of forms, then, under the binary operation induced by detachment, this family is a semigroup having the class of equivalence of Ω as unit element, both left and right. See Clifford and Preston, [1].

Section 1.7 Parametric Detachment

Let us associate to each form $\underline{a}$ an integer parameter $\bar{M}(\underline{a})$ such that

$$\bar{M}(\underline{a}) \geq M(\underline{a}) \qquad (1)$$

Whenever a form $\underline{a}$ is newly introduced without specifying its parameter, this one is taken to be $M(\underline{a})$

Resuming the notation used in section 1.5 to define partial detachment, let us consider the new form obtained from $\underline{b}$ by replacing for $\underline{v}_r$, $(1 \leq \underline{r} \leq \underline{k})$, the new variable letter $(\underline{x}, \underline{i}_r - M(\underline{a}) + \bar{M}(\underline{a}))$ if

$$\underline{i}_r > M(\underline{a}), \qquad (2)$$

or else the $\underline{i}_r$-th canonical component $\underline{a}_{i_r}$ of $\underline{a}$. This new form differs from $(\underline{b} \mid_p \underline{a})$ only by the variable letters satisfying (2), which in this case have a subscript which exceeds the one they would have in $(\underline{b} \mid_p \underline{a})$ by $\bar{M}(\underline{a})-M(\underline{a})$.

This new form is called parametric partial detachment of $\underline{b}$ from $\underline{a}$ with parameter $\bar{M}(\underline{a})$ and denoted

$$\left(\underline{b} \,\Big|_p^{\bar{M}(\underline{a})} \underline{a}\right)$$

and

$$\bar{M}\left(\underline{b} \,\Big|_p^{\bar{M}(\underline{a})} \underline{a}\right) \text{ is defined as}$$

$$\bar{M}(\underline{b}) - M(\underline{a}) + \bar{M}(\underline{a}) \qquad (3).$$

The associativity of partial detachment of forms can be extended to parametric partial detachment of forms, thus obtaining the following

<u>Theorem 1:</u> <u>If $\underline{a}$, $\underline{b}$ and $\underline{c}$ are forms such that</u>

$$M(\underline{b}) \gtrsim M(\underline{a})$$

$$M(\underline{c}) \gtrsim M(\underline{b})$$

$$\bar{M}(\underline{b}) - M(\underline{b}) \gtrsim M(\underline{a})$$

then

$$\left(\underline{c}\,\Big|_p^{\bar{M}(\underline{b}|_p\underline{a})}\;\cdot\;\left(\underline{b}\,\Big|_p^{M(\underline{a})}\,\underline{a}\right)\right) = \left(\left(\underline{c}\,\Big|_p^{M(\underline{b})}\,\underline{b}\right)\Big|_p^{M(\underline{a})}\,\underline{a}\right) \tag{4}$$

<u>Proof</u>: Can be obtained by graphically replacing for each occurrence of M an occurrence of $\bar{M}$ in theorem 2, section 1.5.

An undecomposable form of level ≥ 1 is called <u>normal</u>. The first occurrence $\underline{a}_1$ of a mark in a normal form $\underline{a}$ must be the one of an open parenthesis, otherwise $\underline{a}_2$, which must exist because $\underline{a}$ has level ≥ 1, would have to be the occurrence of depth 0 of a comma and $\underline{a}$ would not be undecomposable. Similarly, the last occurrence of a mark in $\underline{a}$ must be the one of a closed parenthesis. There cannot be in $\underline{a}$ occurrences of marks at depth 0, because this would immediately yield the occurrence at depth 0 of commas.

Consider a structural proof of a normal form $\underline{a}$. The last statement, stating that $\underline{a}$ is a form, cannot be an occurrence of either definition 1 or 2, section 1.2, because in the first case $\underline{a}$ would have level 0 and in the second one it would be decomposable. Therefore this statement must be an occurrence of definition 3, section 1.2, stating that $\underline{a}$ is a form because it results from the enclosure in parentheses of another form $\underline{a}^*$. Consequently, if one

removes the initial open and the final closed parentheses from a normal form $\underline{a}$ we will find another form $\underline{a}^*$. This parentheses removal operation is called peeling, and $\underline{a}^*$ is called interior of $\underline{a}$.

The concept of parametric partial detachment needs some justification. Let $\{\underline{g}_i\}$, $i=1,2..M$, be a sequence of forms, and let $\underline{e}$ be another form such that $M(\underline{e}) = M$ and such that all canonical components of $\underline{e}$ are normal. Consider the form

$$(\underline{g}_1 |_p \underline{e}_1), (\underline{g}_2 |_p \underline{e}_2), \ldots\ldots, (\underline{g}_M |_p \underline{e}_M) \qquad (5)$$

where $\underline{e}_i$ denotes the interior of the $\underline{i}$-th canonical component of $\underline{e}$. In general, $\underline{e}_i$ may be not compact, and it can happen for up to all values of $\underline{i}$ but one, that $M(\underline{e}_i) < M(\underline{e})$. If this happens and $M(\underline{g}_i) < M(\underline{e}_i)$, then the i-th component of the form (5) contains occurrences of a variable letter $(\underline{x}, M(\underline{e}_i)+1)$ which is generated by changing the subscript of the variable letter $(\underline{x}, M(\underline{e}_i)+1)$ occurring in $\underline{g}_i$. Let now $\underline{e}_j$ be such that $M(\underline{e}_j) = M(\underline{e})$, and assume that $\underline{e}_j$ is also compact. The j-th component of (5) still contains occurrences of the variable letter $(\underline{x}, M(\underline{e}_j)+1)$, which, however, has a completely different origin, because such occurrences pre-existed in $\underline{e}_j$. This example shows that forms $\underline{g}_i$ are detached from the interior of the corresponding components of another form $\underline{e}$, then the global notational distinction of variable letters can be no longer preserved. However, if (5) is replaced by

$$\left(\underline{g}_1 \Big|^{M(e)}_{p} \underline{e}_1\right), \left(\underline{g}_2 \Big|^{M(e)}_{p} \underline{e}_2\right), \ldots\ldots, \left(\underline{g}_{M(e)} \Big|^{M(e)}_{p} \underline{e}_M\right) \qquad (6)$$

[illegible]

[illegible] threaded [illegible]

[illegible] sometimes called [illegible]

[illegible] investigat[illegible] the use of [illegible] the items of [illegible] organized as sequential or linear threaded lists, without branching points. However, [illegible] the same hierarchy [illegible] a scheme, called [illegible] threading, [illegible]

(the free storage list) as soon as their contents become irrelevant to further processing. Maintenance of this pool is carried out automatically by the abstract computer. The percentage of memory space devoted to organizational overhead is thus constant with respect to the length of the aggregates stored there. As it will be seen in the sequel, also the percentage of time devoted to overhead operations, such as addressing, is also constant with respect to the length of the aggregates operated upon. This constant ratio of overhead space and time is an important peculiar feature of this abstract computer, and many aspects of its design have been devised in order to provide it with this feature. The study of computation schemes where the ratio between average organizational overhead in space or time and total space or time, respectively, increases and tends to 1 when the length or the complexity of the information to be processed increases, may have a certain mathematical interest but cannot possibly give good indications for the advancement of the computation methodology. In fact, while a constant overhead ratio, even very high, can potentially be reduced by skillful tailoring, this is not the case for overhead ratios not bounded above by a number < 1. This is, in essence, the angle from which the design of the memory organization of this abstract computer should be viewed.

[illegible]

[illegible]

In [illegible] represent [illegible]

[illegible]

A list is said to be empty [illegible] contain information [illegible]

the [illegible] one of [illegible] [illegible]

the right fields of the words of empty [illegible] regarded as not containing significant information.

In the metalanguage the contents of the three [illegible] of the words of a list are written in three forms [illegible]

For example, the following is the storage diagram of an empty list of 4 words

200	51
51	2
2	100
100	[illegible]

The address of the first and last word of a list (200 and 100, respectively, in the case of the last example) will be referred to as <u>initial address</u> and <u>final address</u> of the list, respectively. The first of them is sufficient to identify a list.

Let S_1 and S_2 be two lists having no words having common addresses. The <u>addition of S_1 to S_2</u> is a new list S_3 of $N(S_1) + N(S_2)$ words consisting of the first $N(S_1) - 1$ words of S_1, followed by the last word of S_1 with the initial address of S_2 replacing the contents of its left field, followed by all words of S_2. The initial and final address of S_3 are those of S_1 and S_2, respectively. Addition of lists, whenever possible, is clearly associative.

If $\underline{w}$ is either a word of a list or the address of a word of a list, then $\mathcal{L}\,\underline{w}$, $\mathcal{C}\,\underline{w}$, and $\mathcal{R}\,\underline{w}$ denote the contents of the left, centre and right field of $\underline{w}$ or of the word having $\underline{w}$ as address, respectively. Furthermore, notations such as $\mathcal{L}\mathcal{L}\,\underline{w}$ or $\mathcal{R}\mathcal{R}\mathcal{R}\,\underline{w}$ will be shortened into $\mathcal{L}^2\underline{w}$ or $\mathcal{R}^3\underline{w}$, respectively.

[illegible]

n_2-th, [illegible] n_2-th word has [illegible] address of this section are the one of the [illegible] n_2-th word of S, respectively. Let S' denote this n_1-n_2 section of S. The n_1-n_2 remainder of S [illegible] belonging to [illegible] replaced by the address of the [illegible] The initial [illegible] or the one of its (n_2+1)-th word, depending on whether or not $n_2 \geq 1$, while its final address [illegible] its (n_1-1)-th word, according [illegible] or not n_2 [illegible]

[illegible]

If w_1 and w_2 are [illegible] n_2-th word of a list S, [illegible] remainder [illegible] respectively. In those cases [illegible] n_1 and n_2 are not

The notations n_1-section, n_1-remainder, w_1 address section and w_1-address remainder are used for [illegible], etc.

[illegible] the n_1-th word [illegible] address n_1 [illegible] the end of the list involved.

Certain lists which ones [illegible] need a permanent reference [illegible] [illegible] a word called control word [illegible] This word will also have three fields, [illegible] the [illegible] of the list. [illegible] the control word [illegible] of the [illegible] by a horizontal line. For example, if the [illegible] has a control word located in address 29, [illegible] represented [illegible]

29	200
200	91
91	0
0	100
100	0

The control word of a 0-list contains a 0 in [illegible]

Section 2.2 Aggregates in Lists

Let S be a list, a an aggregate and n a positive integer, such that

$$L(a) \leq n + N(S) - 1 \qquad (1)$$

Let a_i $(i=1,2,\ldots,L(a))$ denote the i-th occurrence of a mark in a. If for all i the mark occurring in a_i is located in the centre field of the $(n + L(a) - i - 1)$-th word of S, then the aggregate a is said to be n-allocated in the list S. If w is the address of the n-th word of S, and a is n-allocated in S, it may also be said to be w-address allocated in S. Notice that aggregates are allocated in lists in the reverse order, in the sense that the highest occurrence of a mark goes into the n-th word, etc. If n is not mentioned it is taken to be 1. ¶ Given an aggregate a, we wish to extend the definition of depth of an occurrence a_i of a mark in a to the case of occurrences of parentheses. The intuitive meaning of this extension should be that the depth in a of the occurrence a_i of an open or closed parenthesis, respectively, should equal the one of an imaginary additional mark which were introduced to the immediate right or left, respectively, of a_i in a.

In order to extend this concept formally, let us first think in terms of left depth $D_\ell(a_i, a)$. If $i=1$, then its left depth is -1 or +1, depending on whether it is a closed or open parenthesis. For $i > 1$, if a_i is an open parenthesis its left depth is defined as $D_\ell(a_{i-1}, a)+1$. If it is a closed parenthesis, $D_\ell(a_i, a)$ is either $D_\ell(a_{i-1}, a)$ or $D_\ell(a_{i-1}, a)$, depending on whether or not a_{i-1} was the occurrence of a closed parenthesis. Conversely, $D_r(a_{L(a)}, a)$ is 1 or -1 whenever

a_{i} is the occurrence of a closed or open parenthesis, respectively, and $D_r(a_i, a)$, for $i < l(a)$, is $D_r(a_{i+1}, a) - 1$ or $D_r(a_{i+1}, a)$, depending on whether or not a_{i+1} is the occurrence of an open parenthesis. If a is a form, left and right depths thus defined are always equal and never negative.

After reminding that the right depth of occurrences of marks in partial forms can never be negative, let a_i be an occurrence of right depth d of an open parenthesis in the partial form a. Then there must be occurrences of depth d of closed parentheses or commas to the right of a_i in a, and let us call mate of a_i the rightmost of them.

Let us extend this concept of mate to the case where a_i is an occurrence at depth d of a comma in a. If there are in a and to the right of a_i occurrences of commas or closed parentheses of depth d, then the leftmost of them is the mate of a_i. Otherwise, a_i is said to be unmated in a. If a_j is the mate of a_i, then a_i will be called the antimate of a_j. If a contains occurrences of commas of depth 0, the leftmost of them in a is called the initial mate of a. Otherwise, a is said to be initially unmated. Furthermore, if a_i is an occurrence of depth d of a closed parenthesis in a, then, if there exist in a to the left of a_i occurrences of open parentheses at depth d, then rightmost of them is the mate of a_i. Notice that the antimate of the mate of a_i is not necessarily a_i.

For example, in the form [illegible] the mate of [illegible]

the mate of [illegible] $(, B, ($ [illegible]

/ the occurrence of the open parenthesis [illegible] occurrence [illegible]

V

comma, the mate of the [illegible] of a comma is the occurrence of the closed [illegible], while the first occurrence of a comma is unmated. The initial mate of this form is [illegible] first occurrence of a comma. [illegible] closed parenthesis is the [illegible] mate is the occurrence of the open parenthesis.

By means of an argument similar to the one used to prove the canonical decomposition theorem one can easily prove that the aggregate consisting of [illegible] in a form included between an occurrence of a mark and its mate, exclusive of extremes, or [illegible] are forms.

[illegible]

of the (n-1)-th word of S or the [illegible] of the control word of S, depending on whether or not n > 1. If $n+L(n)-1 \leq N(S)$, suppose further that the [illegible] field of the $(n+L(n))$-th word of S contains the address of the word of S carrying the initial [illegible], or, if n is initially unmated, the address of [illegible] if n > 1 or the one of the control word of S [illegible], suppose that the above address is contained in a special word associated with S, called [illegible], which will be discussed in section 2.3.

[illegible] has the [illegible]

[illegible] [illegible] the [illegible] [illegible] parenthesis [illegible] when one is brought to [illegible] which [illegible] field [illegible] the [illegible] on the last occurrence of [illegible] of the g [illegible] of g if one does the same [illegible] for [illegible] from a word [illegible] occurrence g_i of [illegible] parenthesis in g, then one is brought to a [illegible] in its [illegible] field the end of the end of the p-[illegible] [illegible] of the form included [illegible] [illegible] of the [illegible] whole form, are [illegible] contain this information relevant to their [illegible] of [illegible] and [illegible] form [illegible] rapid [illegible] to the component [illegible] of components [illegible] the [illegible] of [illegible] right field are called [illegible] of the [illegible] contents of the left fields, called [illegible] or [illegible], allow for scanning forms in sequence, one occurrence of a mark after the other. While the average [illegible] of [illegible] the occurrence of a mark through the [illegible] is [illegible] proportional to the depth of each [illegible] and does not depend on the length of the form involved, [illegible] of doing it through physical [illegible] is proportional to the length of the form. The only [illegible] of adopting

[illegible]

[illegible] aggregate, in [illegible] the forms, have in [illegible] only [illegible] varying length [illegible] be realized by threading [illegible] of the abstract computer is determinant, and [illegible] efficient sequential storage allocation. The position of logical threading is quite different; in fact, this feature of the abstract computer allows it to record canonical components of forms directly and thus protects attachments efficiently. Because of logical threading, the rate of overhead operations due to addressing in the abstract computer is independent of the size of the aggregates on which it operates, so that complex forms are treated as easily as simple ones. In contrast, addressing of components of forms based on physical threading, while beyond any doubt would be logically [illegible], would imply a ratio of overhead operations for addressing purposes strongly increasing with the size of the aggregates operated upon. Such a solution would be against the basic assumptions of the design of the abstract computer.

It should also be noticed that, while physical threading moves always backwards through forms imbedded in lists, logical threading moves forward, with the only exception of when occurrences of closed parentheses are encountered. ¶As previously said, words of memory are always divided in three fields, of which the central one should

[illegible] the [illegible] of the [illegible]

[illegible] the [illegible] of the [illegible]

[illegible]

[illegible] partial forms in logical lists. [illegible] which was [illegible] section 2.2 [illegible] on the alloca- [illegible] was concerned

[illegible] of S [illegible] the [illegible] of S consisting [illegible] address is [illegible]

[illegible] S contains [illegible] n [illegible], the r-th [illegible] of n [illegible] in S. The [illegible] of q is [illegible] of the logical list.

[illegible] been defined to consist [illegible] physical threading, is that [illegible] reverse order, and the end

for physical threading is the beginning for logical threading. The units of information on which the abstract computer operate are forms and their canonical components, not marks, and when canonical components of a form a imbedded in a logical list ℓ are to be operated upon the i-th of them is found [illegible] immediately, since its rightmost occurrence of a mark is [illegible] [illegible]. The addressing system of the abstract computer is based on logical threading, and one should think of a logical list a in terms of a list or lists of lists, etc., linked by the logical threading rather than in terms of a list of words linked by physical threading. The sole purpose of physical threading is to achieve maximum utilization of physical storage, and the reason why it goes backwards with respect to logical threading only depends on the mode of operation of the abstract computer which, as it will be explained in chapter 3, must read the forms backwards in order to evaluate them.

In the metalanguage the contents of the top pointer of logical lists will always be displayed on a line at the end, separated from the contents of the words of the list by a horizontal rule.

In the sequel, a list other than a logical list will be referre to as physical list. Physical lists are not suitable to carry structured information such as partial forms, and their main usage is connected with storing and addressing in sequence marks, mainly constants.

Section 2.8. Imbedding with an Auxiliary List

Under the assumption that all of storage available for allocating marks is originally in the free storage list, no problems should arise as far as the maintenance of physical threading is concerned. In fact, additions, erasures and relocations described above are all operations which preserve physical threading. But this is not the case of logical threading, unless something is done about it. The scheme discussed in this section allows to solve this problem by associating to each logical list S another list U, called sequencing list of S, such that the logical items allocated in it are not aggregates but simply marks, so that physical threading can be exceptionally used also for addressing purposes. An algorithm to produce the logical threading of partial forms imbedded in logical list is thus defined in terms of the allocation of marks into a physical list.

The operation of the simple physical list referred to as U in this section is at all similar to the one of devices, sometimes called push down lists or stacks, which are present in programmed forms in most program compilers for conventional computers and in wired form in certain semi-conventional computers. Such lists are lists of marks, not of structured information, and therefore can be physically addressed. On the other hand, the logical lists used by this abstract computer are a more general concept, for which there is no intuitive equivalent in conventional or semi-conventional machines.

Let $\underline{a}$ be a partial form and $\underline{a}_i$ the $\underline{i}$-th occurrence from the right of a mark in $\underline{a}$. The first thing to do is to devise a simple algorithm for associating to each $\underline{a}_i$ its right depth. For this purpose, one utilizes a sequence $\underline{b}_j$, $(j=0,1 \ldots L(\underline{a}))$ of numbers and a sequence $\underline{c}_j$ of truth values defined as follows:

$$\underline{b}_0 = 0$$

$$\underline{b}_i = \begin{cases} \underline{b}_{i-1} + 1, & \text{whenever } \underline{a}_i \text{ is the occurrence of a closed parenthesis} \\ \underline{b}_{i-1} - 1, & \text{whenever } \underline{c}_{i-1} \text{ has the value } \tau \\ \underline{b}_{i-1} & \text{otherwise} \end{cases}$$

while

$$\underline{c}_0 = \gamma$$

$$\underline{c}_i = \begin{cases} \tau & \text{whenever } \underline{a}_i \text{ is the occurrence of an open parenthesis} \\ \gamma & \text{otherwise} \end{cases}$$

The purpose of the definitions is to be able, for all $\underline{i}$, to compute the integer $D_r(\underline{a}_i, \underline{a})$, which equals $\underline{b}_i$, on the basis of information pertaining to $\underline{a}_i$ and $\underline{a}_{i-1}$ alone.

Let us consider the problem of proceeding from the partial form $\underline{a}$ to generating a logical list S with top pointers and control word $\underline{\ }$ such that N(S) = L($\underline{a}$), in which a is 1-imbedded. The basic tool for this operation is a list U, which initially consists of just one word, containing in its centre field the address of $\underline{s}_0$. The list S is initially a $\underline{0}$-list, consequently both $\mathcal{L}^{top}_{0} = 0$ and $\mathcal{L}_{0} = \mathcal{L}^{top}_{0}$ = address of $\underline{s}_0$. The algorithm consists of L($\underline{a}$) steps each

of which starts with the computation of $\underline{b}_i$ and $\underline{m}_i$ and the addition to the end of S of the mark $\underline{m}_i$ occurring in $\underline{a}_i$: this implies the replacement of $\mathcal{L}\,\underline{s}_\omega$ by the previous contents of the left field of the control word of the free storage list.

Let $\underline{u}_j$ denote the j-th word of U. Then, if $\underline{m}_i$ is a closed parenthesis, a new word, carrying $\underline{m}_i$ in its centre field and the address $\mathcal{L}\,s_\omega$ of the i-th word of S in its right field is added to the beginning of U. If $\underline{m}_i$ is a comma, $\mathcal{R}\,\underline{u}_1$ is placed into the right field of the i-th word of S, whose address is $\mathcal{L}\,\underline{s}_\omega$: then, if $\mathcal{C}\,\underline{u}_1$ is a comma, $\mathcal{R}\,\underline{u}_1$ is replaced by $\mathcal{L}\,s_\omega$, while, if $\mathcal{C}\,\underline{u}_1$ is a closed parenthesis, a new word, carrying $\underline{m}_i$ in its centre field and $\mathcal{L}\,s_\omega$ in its right field is added to the beginning of U. If $\underline{m}_i$ is an open parenthesis, $\mathcal{R}\,\underline{u}_1$ is placed into the right field of the i-th word of S; then, if j is the smallest positive integer such that $\mathcal{C}\,\underline{u}_j$ is a closed parenthesis, $\mathcal{L}\,s_\omega$ is placed into the right field of the word of U having $\mathcal{R}\,\underline{u}_j$ as address; finally, the first j words of U are erased and given back to free storage. In all other cases no further action is taken. At the end of the performance of the algorithm, U contains as many words as the difference between the number of occurrences of open and closed parentheses in $\underline{a}$, plus 1.

Consider now the problem of proceeding from the above logical list with $\underline{a}$ 1-imbedded in it to another logical list S' resulting from adding a partial expression $\underline{a}'$ to the end of S. This operation can be

easily performed provided that the status of U at the end of the generation of S, the integer $b_{L(a)}$ which is the length of U minus one, and the truth value $t_{L(a)}$ which is $\frac{t}{0}$ [illegible] the $s_{L(a)}$ is a closed parenthesis, are available. In fact, S' can be generated just by continuing the operation of forming S beyond the L(a)-th step, considering a' as extension of a.

This procedure shows the relevance to the operations of any logical list S of three items, namely the list U, the registers b and t which at each step contain the right depth b_i and the constant t_i, respectively. List U is called associated list of S, while the compound of b and t, which, for all purposes, can be placed in the same word of memory, is called the associated depth register of S and denoted R_d.

The above basic procedure can be trivially extended to   n-imbeddings of partial forms a into logical lists S such that N(S)   n + L(a) - 1.

From this point on, if a capital Roman character with or without superscripts denotes a list, the corresponding lower case character with the same superscripts and an integer subscript i will be denoted the i-th word of that list if i   0, or its control word if i=0. The symbolic subscript   is used to identify the top pointer. For example, if S is a list, then s_0 is its control word, s_5 its fifth word and $s_{[illegible]}$ its top pointer.

Section 2.[illegible] [illegible] of [illegible]

There will be need for an addition to the logical threading system, [illegible] of the abstract [illegible] in order to [illegible] [illegible] is rather awkward [illegible] this addition, consisting of the backward [illegible] of the conditional [illegible] [illegible] information [illegible].

[illegible] that [illegible] If there is no such [illegible] $\underline{e}_i$ [illegible] [illegible], however, are of little or no relevance to computation). For example, the [illegible] of the occurrence of [illegible] in the form

$$[illegible] (\underline{x}, 2), (\underline{x}, 3), [illegible] \quad (1)$$

is the second occurrence of [illegible] from the left. Notice that the

contains in its right field the address of the $\underline{i}$-th word of the list S, while the first one contains in its right field the right depth $\underline{R}_i$ of $\underline{a}_i$ and in its center field $\underline{a}_i$. If $\underline{a}_i$ is a comma, then, if both $\rho_\lambda \underline{u}_i^0 \neq \underline{b}_i$ and $\rho_\lambda \underline{u}_i^1 \neq \underline{b}_i$, no action is taken. If $\rho_\lambda \underline{u}_i^1 = b_i$, $\underline{v}_i = \gamma$ and $\xi \underline{u}_i^1 = \delta_1^*$, this means that $\underline{a}_i$ is the mate of the occurrence of δ_1^* whose address is $\xi \underline{u}_i^1$, and the action to be taken consists of placing the address of the $\underline{i}$-th word of S into the left field of the word of S whose address is $\xi \underline{u}_i^1$, and then removing the first two words of U^1 (that is, replacing U by the 2-remainder of U).

Another possibility is that $\underline{b}_i = \rho_\lambda \underline{u}_i^0$, $\underline{v}_i = \gamma$ and $\xi \underline{u}_i^0 = \delta_0^*$. This case is analogous to the first one, with the only difference that $\underline{a}_i$ is the mate of an occurrence of a δ_0^* instead of δ_1^*. The action to be taken is exactly the one of the first case, with the only difference that δ_0^* and U^0 replace δ_1^* and U^1, respectively.

Finally, if neither of these two combinations of conditions is satisfied, $\underline{a}_i$ is not the mate of anything and no action is taken.

The basic difference between the operations of mating occurrences of open parentheses or commas on one side and occurrences of closed parentheses, δ_0^* and δ_1^* on the other for imbedding purposes is that in the first case one should memorize all addresses of possible mates and place them when the occurrence to be mated is found, while in the second case, since the occurrence of closed parentheses and condition marks

[illegible]

Notice also that, [illegible] [illegible] [illegible] it is not necessary [illegible] [illegible] possible [illegible] [illegible] [illegible] [illegible] [illegible] section [illegible]

For example the form

END, [illegible]

can be [illegible] embedded in a [illegible] as follows.

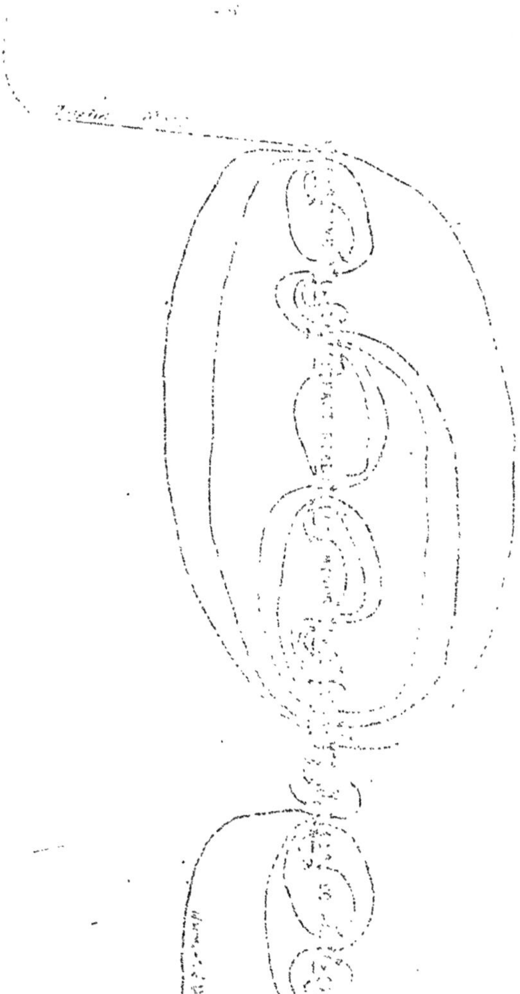

 15-63

 16-63

 17-63

 18-63

 19-63

 20-63

 21-63

 22-63

no item for 140

www.ingramcontent.com/pod-product-compliance
Lightning Source LLC
Chambersburg PA
CBHW071217050326
40689CB00011B/2352
9781014941534